for
My Little Bear and Bean.
You are the loves of my life.

Tiny Dots
for
Tiny Tots

Loom knit toys for
girls and boys!

by

Kelly E. Jones

Permission requests may be sent to the author at the following address:

Tiny Dots
1214 Walnut Street
Murphysboro, IL 62966

Author & Designer:
  Kelly E Jones

Illustrators:
  Bill Guthridge
  Darryl T Jones

Photography:
  Kelly E Jones

Project Editors:
  Linda Nelson
  Kathy Bouras

Text Editor:
  Laura Baird

Models:
  Ruth Jones
  Isaiah Jones
  Cliff Roush

Graphic Designer:
  Darryl T Jones

ISBN:
  978-1481048507
  1481048503

First U.S. Edition: March 2013

Tiny Dots *for* Tiny Tots

Table of Contents

My story begins in 2007 after my son was born. I had received a number of homemade knit blankets from friends and family and felt a desire to make him a blanket all on my own. At the time I thought I would learn to needle knit, but I met this wonderful retired school teacher at Hobby Lobby who not only explained to me that a skein was a ball of yarn (I really WAS a newbie), she showed me the looms and told me how easy it was. I'm forever grateful to her for her kind instruction and I have been looming ever since!

In 2009 my story picks up with Kiss Looms. Cliff Roush, owner of Kiss Looms, contacted me to redo his website (my husband and I own Splattered Ink, a website development company). Cliff and I instantly connected with one another and through doing the website became the best of friends. It's funny that Cliff started inventing Kiss Looms around the same time that I started looming in 2007. Having never tried a Kiss Loom, he sent me one and I simply fell in love with it. I truly believe it's the most versatile loom you can use. Cliff and I kept working together even after the website was done and I started helping with marketing and sales.

Early 2010 brought some health concerns to Cliff and in an effort to protect Kiss Looms we came up with a plan for my dad and I to help make looms. So we spent the next year or so learning even more about the looms and how to make them. Over the course of 2012 looms were being made by both my dad and Cliff. In Nov 2012 Cliff decided to go ahead and turn the loom making over to dad and me full time, and I'm sorry to say that Cliff passed away on Christmas Eve 2012. His loss is felt greatly.

So 2013 starts a new chapter for me as I publish this book and learn the loom making trade. It's been a strange and wonderful 7 years and left me in a place that only God knew I wanted and needed to be. I've been married to the love of my life for over 12 years and have two of the most wonderful, beautiful, gifted children. They inspire me to do great things.

My hope for you is that whether you are brand new to looming or an old hat that you'll love this hobby and way of life for a very long time. It can lead you to people and places you never could have imagined.

God bless you, and happy looming!

Kelly E. Jones

An Introduction to Kiss Looms

The Kiss Looms are very different from traditional knitting looms because they are gauge adjustable. I'll spend a little time explaining some of the basics, but you should also check out the tutorials section on the Kiss Loom website for more information.

Kiss Looms use a peg and pin system to achieve different gauges in your knitting. Each loom has two boards – a peg board and a pin board. The pin board is what is used to determine the gauge of your knitting. When you are wrapping a row, you wrap in front of one peg, behind the pin then in front of the second peg and repeat. Always make sure you go behind the pin before going to the next peg. The distance the yarn travels from peg to peg increases the further you move the pin board from the peg board. This is what changes the gauge of your knitted fabric. You place washers between the two boards on the bolts to increase the distance between the peg and pin boards.

On a traditional loom the pegs are permanently set further apart so you need a different loom for each gauge you'd like to achieve. With the Kiss Loom you can knit with no washers for the smallest gauge or add up to the 7 included washers to equal the KK gauge. This makes Kiss Looms the most versatile loom available. The great thing about the peg and pin system is that it has a side effect of making nice even stitches and you can wrap the whole row with a u-wrap stitch before knitting off.

What is a U-Wrap?

A u-wrap is a knit stitch that forms the traditional v-shaped stitches of a stockinette fabric (all knit stitches). The difference is that with the pin system you can wrap the entire row then knit off. This is similar to the technique of the e-wrap on the KK's EXCEPT that you get the nice v-shaped stitch. An e-wrap is also called a twisted knit stitch because it is literally twisted. It forms a larger y-shaped stitch.

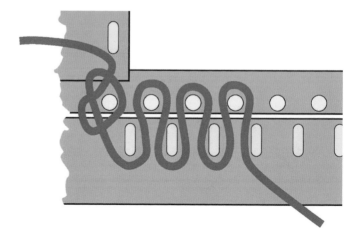

Types of Kiss Looms

What is a 2-Way Adjustable?

The looms are adjustable in 2 different ways. One way is the adjustable gauge by adding or subtracting washers. The other way it is adjustable is by number of pegs to knit in the round. Our end pieces, whether a single peg slider or the larger ends can be be moved back and forth across the sides to change the number of pegs to knit. With the 1 peg sliders you can move it all the way down to one end to knit a 4 peg i-cord in the round.

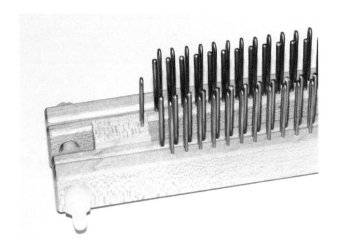

What is a Modular Loom?

A modular loom also has the gauge adjustable feature as do most of our looms but has a fixed number of pegs for knitting in the round. The great thing about the modular looms is that you can build a larger loom using the straight and corner brackets. Simply attach the modulars together into any number of pegs you need whether you are knitting a flat panel or knitting in the round. Want to knit a king size blanket in one panel? This is the loom for you!

What is a Fixed Loom?

The fixed looms are the only ones that are not gauge adjustable. In order to get the small gauge needed for sock yarns the pegs and pins must be on the same board. Remember, the pin system is what makes for a nice even stitch and allows you to wrap the whole row before knitting off. There are two types of fixed looms - fixed 1 and fixed 2. The fixed 1 is the smallest gauge you can get on a Kiss Loom. The fixed 2 is a slightly larger gauge and bridges the gap between the fixed 1 and small gauge looms.

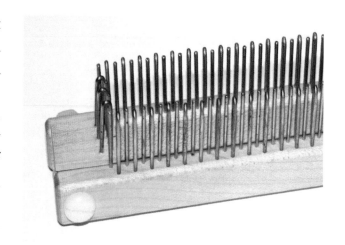

How To Set Up Your Kiss Loom

To set up your Kiss Loom for the projects in this book you will be using the smallest setting which is 0 washers. You will be using 24 pegs for the body of the projects. The illustration shows the location for the 1 peg sliders. Each peg has a partner pin to

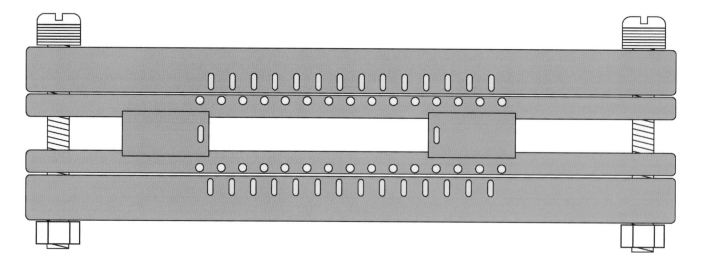

the left and right. The end slider pegs will be lined up with the pins on the outside edges of the number of pegs used. So for example, the slider on the left in the picture is lined up on the outside pins at one end of the loom. There are 11 pegs on top and bottom. The right hand slider is lined up on the partner pin on the right side of the 11th peg.

Note: When you are using washers on the loom, these end sliders will need to move outward to match the distance of the traveling yarn on the sides. The traveling yarn is how much yarn is used from the front of a peg to the front of another peg after it goes behind the partner pin. Increasing and decreasing the amount of the traveling yarn by adding and subtracting washers

is what changes the size (gauge) of your stitches. If you are using the end pieces for this loom, you will always line up the pins on the sides with the pins on the ends. Just make sure you have the same number of washers between the boards on both the ends and sides.

Another setting for the loom you'll need for the patterns in this book is the 4-peg i-cord in the round setting. Again, you will line up the slider pegs with the outside partner pins on the sides. The distance in the middle will be small so you'll need to pull down on the tail and i-cord as you knit. If it's a little too tight you can move the sliders out slightly to allow a little more room.

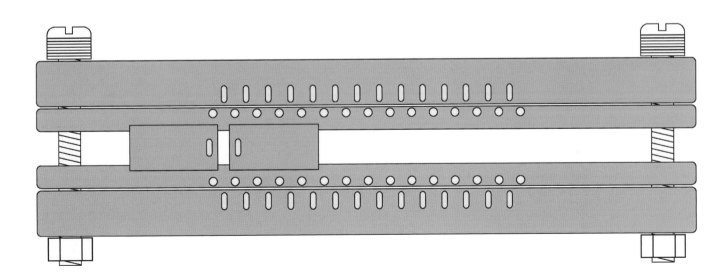

Abbreviations:

K - knit with the u-wrap stitch unless otherwise noted

P – purl

CO – cast on, use dbl ew co unless otherwise noted

DSCO – drawstring cast on

BO – bind off, basic bind off or super stretchy bind off as noted

EW – e-wrap

DBL – double, as in dbl e-wrap

K2tog/K3tog – knit two/three together (see general notes)

P2tog/P3tog – purl two/three together (see general notes)

SSK, SSP - slip slip knit/slip slip purl (see general notes)

SLP – slip stitch with working yarn in back– in other words, do not knit it

KO – knit off

General Instruction:

Read Notes Thoroughly Before Beginning Patterns

Recommended loom: Kiss Small Gauge Compact Slim with 1 peg end

Each pattern has specific elements that are talked about in that pattern. Some techniques are used throughout the patterns and can be found in this general instruction section of the book.

Do not slip the first stitch unless pattern calls for it.

Use dbl ew co unless otherwise noted.

Knit with the u-stitch unless otherwise noted.

All About Gauge

It has long been thought that the only way to change the gauge of a single side loom was to change the spacing of the pegs. The Kiss loom has changed that! The peg and pin system allow you to change the gauge of the knitted fabric produced.

Gauge is set by changing how much yarn is used for each stitch. With regular looms this is done by changing the distance between pegs. The Kiss Loom starts out with a small gauge then uses a pin system to increase the distance the yarn travels between pegs. The gauge is determined by this traveling yarn and by adding washers on the looms you increase the amount of traveling yarn - and therefore change the knitted gauge.

Avg Stitches per 1" for Kiss Looms

loom	yarn	ave stitches
Small Gauge +0 washers	R H	4.5 st x 6 r
Small Gauge +2	R H	4.25 st x 6 r
Small Gauge +4	R H	4 st x 5 r
Reg Peg +0 washers	R H	4 st x 7 r
Reg Peg +2	R H	3.5 st x 6 r
Reg Peg +4	R H	3.25 st x 5 r

yarn type	needle rec	yarn weight
Red Heart & Sole Sock Yarn	US 2	1 – super fine
Red Heart Super Saver Yarn	US 8	4 – med worsted

This chart shows the average number of stitches per 1" that you can get by changing the peg style of the loom or simply by changing the number of washers between the boards. The small gauge loom with 0 washers has an average of 4.5 st and 6 rows per 1". If you add 2 washers between the boards you get 4.25 st per 1". So with 2 washers your stitches will increase one quarter of a stitch over 1". This may not seem like much, but let's say you are making a kids sweater on 60 pegs. On the loom set with 0 washers you would have a piece of fabric 13.33" wide. The loom with 2 washers would be 14.11" wide. If you used 4 washers you would have a 15" wide piece of fabric. You can see that this could really make a difference in your finished item. The rows per 1" don't change on the first two examples, but change slightly on the 4-washer example. With rows per inch you can easily add or subtract rows to match the size you need.

There are several things that influence the gauge of the knitted fabric.

Loom – different looms will knit differently. The different peg styles on a Kiss loom will have a different gauge.

Yarn – different yarn brands and yarn weights will give you a varying gauge. Even different colors of the same yarn have been known to give a different gauge.

Knitter – each knitter knits a little differently. Some are tight knitters, others are loose, and still others are somewhere in the middle. If a knitter is stressed or relaxed it will also affect gauge.

The best way to determine your gauge is to get your yarn and choose your loom setting and knit a swatch. Then measure the stitches and rows across 4". Measuring across 4" is the standard in most knitting patterns and will give you the best average of your knitting gauge on the swatch. You would then divide the number by 4 to compare to our average stitches and rows per 1".

To measure your gauge you need to lay a metal knitting gauge ruler against your knitted swatch. A metal ruler works best as a fabric or plastic ruler can stretch and cause your measurement to be off. You want to measure in the middle of your swatch, not near the edges. Count the v-shaped stitches horizontally, make sure to count partial stitches too (¼ and ½ stitches). Then count the vertical rows including partial stitches.

Drawstring Cast On (DSCO) in the Round

The drawstring cast on in the round is accomplished by knitting every other peg on the first row, then knitting every peg on the second row. Make sure you always wrap behind the pins. You will then knit off the pegs that have two loops. I always choose a corner pin to place a slip knot on to hold it while doing the cast on. You do not want to slip knot the first peg because you won't be able to gather it closed correctly when you are done.

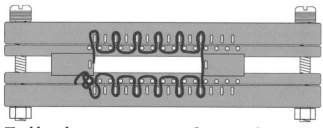

The blue above represents your first row of yarn.

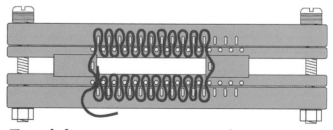

The red above represents your second row of yarn.

Flat Panel DSCO

To do a flat panel drawstring cast on (also called an adjustable cast on by Brenda Myers), you will do something very similar to the DSCO in the round. Wrap every other peg just like you did in the round but when you get to the end peg go to the far side and wrap clockwise around the peg to the front then wrap all the previous pegs. You will only have one loop on every other peg. Knit off the pegs with two loops then begin the pattern instructions.

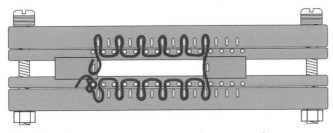

The blue above represents your first row of yarn.

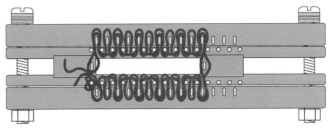

The red above represents your second row of yarn.

Double EW Cast On

I use a double ew cast on most of the time. It is also called a non-loopy cast on. It gives a nice cast on edge that is firm, yet stretchy. Start by placing a slip knot on the first peg and e-wrapping the second peg twice then knit it off. Pull tight a little then go behind the pin and wrap the next peg twice and knit off. Continue in this manner until you cast on the number of pegs required. Just make sure you always go behind the pin before knitting the next peg. There are videos on the Kiss website tutorial page that show how to do this cast on if you need visual instructions.

U-Wrap Stitch

The u-wrap stitch is a knit stitch. It forms the nice traditional v-shaped stitches. It is important to note that this is not a stitch appropriate for a cast on! It would be called an open cast on. In other words, it will unravel unless you have a closed cast on as the previous row. E-wraps and double e-wraps are closed cast on's. To do the u-wrap stitch you wrap in front of the peg and behind the pin, in front of the peg and behind the pin. When you are first learning to knit on a Kiss you'll probably find yourself chanting this to yourself as you go.

As you can see from the illustration your stitches will look like the letter U. The fabric flows down behind the pins. If you accidentally have a loop in front of a pin, just pick it up and lift it over so that it's behind the pin. The fabric won't flow down properly if the loop is in front of the pin. Once the knitting is long enough to flow through the loom you can give the project a little tug after each row and be able to tell if you've caught a loop.

It will not be springy as you pull down. If several rows have passed you can still move this loop and manipulate it back in to the knitting without a problem. If too many rows have passed, you may have lengthened that stitch too much and need to unknit the rows back to that stitch to fix the problem. There are videos of the u-wrap stitch on the Kiss website tutorial section.

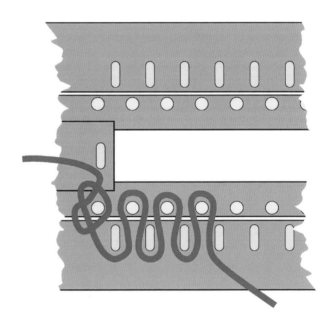

Decreasing

A k2tog or p2tog are a left slanting decrease and loops are always moved to the peg on the left. For example, let's say you have a k2tog, k1, k2tog. Peg 1 is on the right and peg 5 is on the left with working yarn at peg 1. Move peg 1 to 2 and peg 4 to 5. Move the loops on peg 5 back to peg 4 making sure not to twist them or change

the order and making sure you go behind the pin when you move them. Then wrap and knit the row knitting 2 over 1 on those pegs that need it.

A ssk or ssp are a right slanting decrease and are done by moving the loops to the right. Using the example above with peg

1 on the right and peg 5 on the left with working yarn at peg 5, the row says ssk, k1, ssk. You will move peg 5 to 4 and peg 2 to 1. Make sure to close up the gap by moving the loops on peg 1 back to peg 2 making sure not to twist them or change the order. Make sure you go behind the pin when you move the loops over. Then wrap and knit the row knitting 2 over 1 on those pegs that need it.

If you have a row that is mixed using both ssk and k2tog then you will move those pegs in the same matter above for each type of decrease. For example a k2tog, k1, ssk will have you moving peg 1 to 2 and 5 to 4 before wrapping and knitting off. There will be no gaps to close up in this example.

On a 3 peg decrease always move the loop closest to the working yarn last so that it's on top of the other loops. For example: K1, K3tog, K1– knit peg 1, move peg 4 to 3 then 2 to 3 knit 3 over 1, then knit peg 5. On these it's easiest to go ahead and knit the first peg then slip peg 2 and knit the K3tog and move the new loop over to peg 2, pulling it snug to take out the slack from the slipped stitch. Then move peg 5 over and knit it.

How to change colors mid row

When changing colors in the middle of a row you will need to twist the stitches at the back of the work. You will use this method in the tiger pattern for the striped back. On this pattern you will knit the orange stitches then switch to black. When you get to the final orange stitch knit it off and then place the black slip knot on the peg you just knit (this is a a temporary placement – you will remove it without knitting it later). Drop the orange working yarn and knit the black part of the row. On the next row when you get to the final black stitch you will knit it off, remove the slip knot of black from the previous row, pick up the orange yarn and bring it under the black working yarn around to the top and pull it snug and knit the rest of the row in orange. Always twist the yarn with the color you are starting to the top – see photo on the next page (the orange is to the top and you will start knitting the orange on the peg to the right).

The next row will be all in orange. When you get to the section of black, twist the yarn again and complete the row in orange. Do not cut the black yarn between color changes. Each time you come to a color change make sure you twist the yarn but do not pull too tight. When you are done you will want to make sure you tuck the starting and ending tails in really well or it will form a hole in those locations.

How to sew facial features

The main thing to remember is to work in small increments and that if you don't like it you can always change it. The face is an important feature and you need to be happy with the results. Sometimes it takes a few tries before you get one you like.

There are a few different methods for putting the facial features on. There are some great resources for this online too. I highly recommend taking a look at Mochimochi Land for a thorough tutorial (mochimochi-land.com/2008/07/eye-eye-a-tutorial/)

Determine how big you want your eye. For this small project you typically want to use 1-1 ½ stitches. For eyes you can do either a horizontal eye or a vertical eye. Both will look slightly different depending on the shape of the animal. Thread your needle and going in from the side of the ball bring the yarn up at one side of the eye. Put the needle down through the project 1 or 1½ stitches over and back up through your original hole. You will continue this horizontal line eye typically 3-4 times until you have the desired look. Make sure you count so that you can do it the same number of times on the second eye. The more times you do it the more rounded the eye will become. After you finish with that eye, take your yarn through the center of the ball to the second eye location and complete the second eye. To secure the end - thread the needle back and forth through the ball a few times going through the same hole each time – the stuffing and hose will help secure it in place.

For the beaver and raccoon noses I did a longer horizontal line 2-3 times then a vertical line 2-3 times for a slightly different shape.

Back Stitch Method:

For the mouth of the dots it is best to use the sewn back stitch method. You can find many videos online that show this method clearly. Let's say you are forming the mouth right to left. First you will bring the yarn up at the location you want the mouth to start (S) then bring it down two stitches over to the left (a) and underneath two more stitches to the left (b). You then bring the needle down through the hole of the previous stitch (a) filling in the line you missed and underneath 4 stitches to the left (c). Continue in this manner until the mouth shape is formed. It is important to keep the stitches the same length.

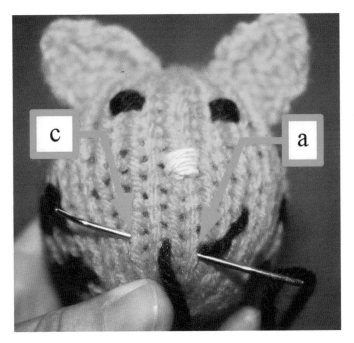

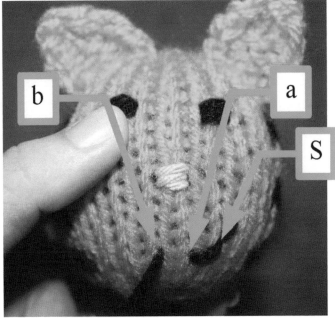

How to knit a flat panel i-cord

When knitting a flat panel i-cord you do not knit back and forth like regular knitting. I typically cast on from right to left. You then go behind all the pins and pegs back to the right hand side (a) and do a u-wrap stitch from right to left (b), knit off starting with the pegs on the edges, then knit off the middle pegs. Go behind all the pins and pegs again to the right hand side (a). You do this each time. Pull down after each row and you will see the gap on the back side close up, forming a rounded i-cord.

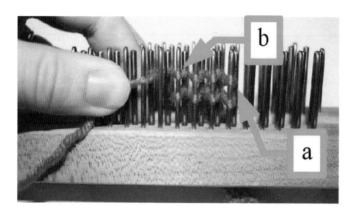

2-Peg I-Cord

Place a slip knot on peg 1 then wrap behind the pin to the right and around the right side of the second peg then around to the left front as if to e-wrap. Go behind the pin to the left and behind the first peg to the left side and around the front to the right. Go behind the pin again and around the right side of the second peg around to the left front. There will be two wraps on each peg and it will look like a figure eight pattern from the top. Knit off these pegs – this is row 1. Continue to wrap in this manner till you have two wraps on the pegs and then knit off.

Raccoon Grey Eye Patch

First sew an outline using the back stitch method described in the notes section. Once the outline is done, begin filling in the middle of the eye patch a little bit at a time until the white is gone. Then stitch the black eye in place.

Cut your working yarn and thread the tail on a yarn needle. Bring your working yarn behind the pins to the opposite end of your working yarn then sew up through each loop on the loom. No need to worry about the pins, just sew to the front of the pegs, making sure you always sew through the loops in the same direction. When you get to the end you are done, pull the project off the loom and drawstring it snugly and secure ends.

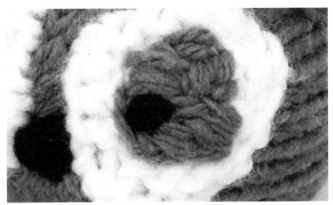

Crochet Chain

Put a slip knot on your crochet hook. Don't make it too tight or it will be hard to pull the next loop through. Push the slip knot back from the hook and lay the working yarn over the end. Pull the working yarn through the slip knot, making a new loop on the hook. Wrap the hook with the working yarn again and pull through. Continue in this manner until the chain is the desired length.

Flat Panel Gather BO

Cut your working yarn and thread the tail on a yarn needle. Bring your working yarn behind the pins to the opposite end of your working yarn then sew up through each loop on the loom. No need to worry about the pins, just sew to the front of the pegs, making sure you always sew through the loops in the same direction. When you get to the end you are done, pull the project off the loom and drawstring it snugly and secure ends.

Basic BO

The key to doing a good basic bind off is to keep it loose! If you are at all afraid you will be too tight, the super stretchy bind off is a better way to go. To do this bind off you will wrap the first and second pegs with the u-stitch. Knit them off then move the second loop on to the first peg as show in the second photo and knit the bottom loop over the top (do not wrap again). Next move the peg one loop over to the empty peg two. Wrap the next peg with a u-stitch then knit off and move the loop to the previous peg. Knit the bottom over the top and move the loop in again. Continue in this manner until you are down to two pegs. You will knit the last peg and knit off, then move it to the previous peg. Knit off bottom over top then cut your working yarn, leaving a 5-8" tail. Grab the last loop on the peg and pull on it until the tail comes through. To finish, snug the end up (it will form what feels like a small knot).

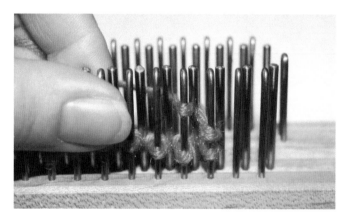

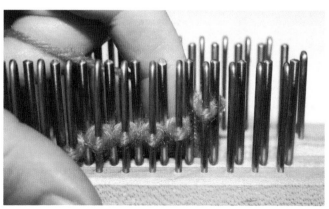

Super Stretchy Bind Off (aka sewn bind off)

The super stretchy bind off is a good pairing with a double e-wrap cast on. It gives a nice firm, but stretchy edge. To do this bind off you will measure the working yarn till it is three times the length of the number of pegs used then cut it. Thread the end through a yarn needle. I prefer a bent tapestry needle as I think it's a little easier to use. To sew your project closed you'll only be working to the front of your loom. This is the only time you won't go behind the pins. With the working yarn held to the front of the loom take the needle up through the loop on the second peg. Next put your needle down through the loops on the first peg. Then you will go up through the loop on the third peg and down through the loops on the second peg. Continue in this manner until you have gone up through the last peg and down through the second-to-last peg. You will go up through the last peg one more time then pull the project off the loom. Voila, you are done. There are two super stretchy bind off videos shown on the Kiss website tutorials page that should help with additional visual instructions.

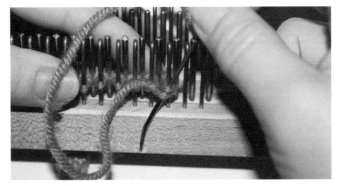
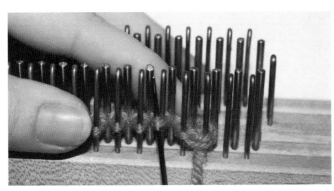
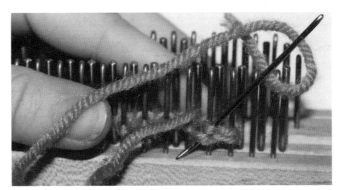

FISH

Whether you knit this fish up for the little ones or big ones in your life I'm sure they'll love it. You can rotate the tail horizontally and add a few more rows to make it a whale tail.

Materials
24 Peg Small Gauge Knitting Loom

Yarn (3) or (4)
20 yards for body and tail. 2 yards for facial features. Red Heart was used in sample.

Tools/Notions
Knitting Pick

Tapestry Needle

Stuffing

Knee Highs or Pantyhose to contain stuffing – choose complimentary color to body of animal

Optional: 30 mm Bell or 1.5" Rattle Noise Maker

Gauge
4.5 st x 5 rows = 1"

Finished Size
Approximately 8" in diameter

BODY • • • • • • • • • • • • • • • • •

DSCO 24 pegs, knit 20 rows in the round, gather bo. Secure one end of body then stuff stocking lightly and knot closed. Insert stocking into body. Gather the end of the body closed and secure yarn tail.

TAIL: MAKE 2 •

Row 1-3, side 1: co 3 pegs, knit 3 rows, cut yarn

Row 1-3, side 2: skip 4 pegs and co 3 pegs back towards side 1, knit 3 rows

Row 4: k3, co 1, k3 (7 pegs total)

Row 5: k

Row 6: k2, k3tog, k2 (5 pegs total)

Row 7: k, k3tog, k (3 pegs total)

Row 8: co 1, k4, co 1 – do not slp first co peg (5 pegs total)

Row 9: k, co 1 (6 pegs total)

Row 10: k, co 1 (7 pegs total)

Row 11: k

Bind off using super stretchy bind off

ASSEMBLY • • • • • • • • • • •

Sew tail pieces together and lightly stuff or use tail ends as stuffing before closing end. Stitch the tail in place on one end of the drawstring ball pulling it out so that it is rounded slightly to meet the shape of the body. Flatten body so that it is a disk shape. Using black yarn stitch the eyes on both sides of the head and mouth across the front and sides using the method described in the notes section.

OWL

No matter whooooooo you're knitting this for, it will be a fun compliment to any of the animals in this book.

Materials

24 Peg Small Gauge Knitting Loom

Yarn (3) or (4)

20 yards for body and wings. 2 yards each for facial features. Lion Brand Wool Ease and Vanna's Choice was used in sample.

Tools/Notions

Knitting Pick

Tapestry Needle

Stuffing

Knee Highs or Pantyhose to contain stuffing – choose complimentary color to body of animal

Optional: 30 mm Bell or 1.5" Rattle Noise Maker

Gauge

4.5 st x 5 rows = 1"

Finished Size

Approximately 8" in diameter

BODY • • • • • • • • • • • • • • • • •

DSCO 24 pegs, knit 20 rows in the round, use gather bo. Secure one end of body then stuff stocking and knot closed. Insert stocking into body. Gather the end of the body closed and secure yarn tail.

EYES: MAKE 2

CO 3 pegs as flat panel

Row 1: p3, co 1

Row 2: k4, co 1

Row 3: p5

Row 4: k5

Row 5: p5

Row 6: ssk, k, k2tog

Row 7: p3

Row 8: k3tog, pull through and snug

BEAK

Row 1-2: knit a 2 peg i-cord for 2 rows then co 1

Row 3: k3, co 1

Row 4: k4

Row 5: k4

Row 6: ssk, k2tog

Row 7: K2tog, pull through and snug

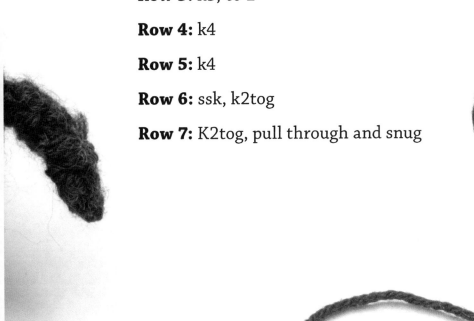

WINGS: MAKE 2

CO 3 pegs as flat panel

Row 1: p3

Row 2: k3, co 1

Row 3: p4, co 1

Row 4: k5

Row 5: p5

Row 6: k5

Row 7: p2tog, p1, ssp

Row 8: k3tog, pull through and snug

ASSEMBLY

Whip stitch the white eyes on, sew on the beak and wings. Using black yarn stitch the eyes in place using the method described in the notes section.

TURTLE

Materials

24 Peg Small Gauge Knitting Loom

Yarn (3) or (4)

20 yards for body and legs.
2 yards for facial features.
Knit Picks Wool of the Andes Tweed was used in sample.

Tools/Notions

Knitting Pick

Tapestry Needle

Stuffing

Knee Highs or Pantyhose to contain stuffing – choose complimentary color to body of animal

Optional: 30 mm Bell or 1.5" Rattle Noise Maker

Gauge

4.5 st x 5 rows = 1"

Finished Size

Approximately 8" in diameter

This turtle is the most realistic looking dot in the book. I used a tweed yarn to really bring out the texture and color of this guy. He came about after finding a big box turtle on our front lawn in the summer. After we released him back at the pond my son needed a little friend to remind him of his turtle friend.

BODY • • • • • • • • • • • • • • • • •

DSCO 24 pegs knit body in the round using the chart. This will form a texture on the top of the turtle

shell. I also chose a tweed yarn for my sample to increase the visual appeal. Use gather bo.

p	k	k	k	k	p	k	k	k	k	p	k	k	k	k	1
p	k	k	k	k	p	k	k	k	k	p	k	k	k	k	2
p	k	k	k	k	p	k	k	k	k	p	k	k	k	k	3
p	k	k	k	k	p	k	k	k	k	p	k	k	k	k	4
p	k	k	k	k	p	k	k	k	k	p	k	k	k	k	5
p	p	p	p	p	p	p	p	p	p	p	p	k	k	k	6
k	k	k	p	k	k	k	k	p	k	k	k	k	k	k	7
k	k	k	p	k	k	k	k	p	k	k	k	k	k	k	8
k	k	k	p	k	k	k	k	p	k	k	k	k	k	k	9
k	k	k	p	k	k	k	k	p	k	k	k	k	k	k	10
p	p	p	p	p	p	p	p	p	p	p	p	k	k	k	11
p	k	k	k	k	p	k	k	k	k	p	k	k	k	k	12
p	k	k	k	k	p	k	k	k	k	p	k	k	k	k	13
p	k	k	k	k	p	k	k	k	k	p	k	k	k	k	14
p	k	k	k	k	p	k	k	k	k	p	k	k	k	k	15
p	p	p	p	p	p	p	p	p	p	p	p	k	k	k	16
k	k	k	p	k	k	k	k	p	k	k	k	k	k	k	17
k	k	k	p	k	k	k	k	p	k	k	k	k	k	k	18
k	k	k	p	k	k	k	k	p	k	k	k	k	k	k	19
k	k	k	p	k	k	k	k	p	k	k	k	k	k	k	20

Before stuffing, start at the top edge near the drawstring bo and whip stitch together 1 ½ stitches on the edge to form the rounded edge for the shell. (See inset graphic.) Stop short of the other drawstring end and stuff stocking lightly and knot closed. Insert stocking into body, flatten body so that it is a disk shape, then pull drawstring closed and secure. Continue seaming the turtle shell edge.

HEAD •

CO 5 pegs as flat panel

Row 1-3: knit 3 rows then co 1

Row 4: k, co 1

Row 5: k1, co 1

Row 6: k1, co 1

Row 7: k

Row 8: ssk, k5, k2tog

Row 9: k2tog, k3, ssk

Row 10: k1, k3tog, k1

Row 11: k3tog, pull through and snug

FEET: MAKE 4

CO 8 pegs in the round, knit 6 rows, use gather bo.

TAIL

Row 1-2: knit 2 peg i-cord for 2 rows then co 1

Row 3: k3, co 1

Row 4: k4

Row 5: k2tog, ssk

Row 6: ssk, pull through and snug

ASSEMBLY

Attach head under the edge of the shell on the bottom. Attach tail to back and legs to sides under the shell edge. Using black yarn, stitch the eyes in place using the method described in the notes section.

PUPPY

Knit this guy up in a variety of colors, with or without the spotted eye. You can even knit up some spots for his back if you like with a couple little spots on his ears.

Materials

24 Peg Small Gauge Knitting Loom

Yarn (3) or (4)

20 yards for body and ears. 2 yards for facial features. I Love This Yarn was used in sample.

Tools/Notions

Knitting Pick

Tapestry Needle

Stuffing

Knee Highs or Pantyhose to contain stuffing – choose complimentary color to body of animal

Optional: 30 mm Bell or 1.5" Rattle Noise Maker

Gauge

4.5 st x 5 rows = 1"

Finished Size

Approximately 8" in diameter

BODY

DSCO 24 pegs, knit 20 rows in the round, use gather bo. Secure one end of body then stuff stocking and knot closed. Insert stocking into body. Gather the end of the body closed and secure yarn tail.

WHITE EYE

CO 3 pegs as flat panel

Row 1: p3, co 1

Row 2: k4, co 1

Row 3: p5

Row 4: k5

Row 5: p5

Row 6: ssk, k, k2tog

Row 7: p3

Row 8: k3tog, pull through and snug

EARS: MAKE 2

CO 8 pegs as flat panel

Row 1: p8, co 1

Row 2: k9

Row 3: p9

Row 4: k9

Row 5: p9 then bo 6 – move loop 8 to 9 ko, move loop back to peg 8, move 7 to 8 ko, move loop back to 7, move loop 6 to 7 ko, move loop back to 6, continue until you have three stitches left

Row 6: k3

Row 7: p3

Row 8: k3

BO: k3tog, pull through and snug

ASSEMBLY

Whip stitch white eye patch and ears in place. Using black yarn stitch the eyes, mouth and nose in place using the method described in the notes section.

BEAVER

This beaver is one of my favorites. The texture in the tail and cute little ears just make this little guy everything I'd hoped for. I hope you enjoy him too.

Materials

24 Peg Small Gauge Knitting Loom

Yarn ③ or ④

25 yards for body, tail and ears. 2 yards for facial features. Red Heart was used in sample.

Tools/Notions

Knitting Pick

Tapestry Needle

Stuffing

Knee Highs or Pantyhose to contain stuffing – choose complimentary color to body of animal

Optional: 30 mm Bell or 1.5" Rattle Noise Maker

Gauge

4.5 st x 5 rows = 1"

Finished Size

Approximately 8" in diameter

BODY •

DSCO 24 pegs, knit 20 rows in the round, use gather bo. Secure one end of body then stuff stocking lightly and knot closed. Insert stocking into body. Gather the end of the body closed and secure yarn tail.

EARS: MAKE 2 •

CO 6 pegs as flat panel

Row 1: slp k

Row 2: slp k

Row 3: k2tog, k2, ssk

Row 4: ssk, k2tog

Row 5: k2tog, pull through and snug

TAIL: MAKE 2

CO 10 pegs as flat panel

Row 1-2: k2, p2, k2, p2, k2

Row 3-4: p2, k2, p2, k2, p2

Repeat these 4 rows till row 16 is complete

Row 17: k2, p2, k2, p2, k2

Row 18: ssk p2, k2, p2, k2tog

Row 19: p, k2, p2, k2, p

Row 20: ssp, k, p2, k, p2tog

Row 21: k2tog, p2, ssk

Bind off using basic BO, pull through and snug

ASSEMBLY

Sew sides and rounded edges of tail together using whip stitch – do NOT seam cast on edges closed. Turn inside out and stuff lightly. Set aside until body is completed. Flatten body so that it is a disk shape. Sew ears in place – make sure they are further back on head. Using black yarn stitch the eyes in place vertically using the method described in the notes section. Referencing the method described in the notes section, stitch the nose in place on the end drawstring area by stitching side to side 4-5 times then top to bottom 2-3 times until you reach desired look. Hold tail cast on edges to body making sure to form it around the body slightly – stitch the tail in place. Tail should not be sewn closed against the body – it should be rounded slightly to meet the shape of the body.

DUCK

Very few ducks actually "quack." Their calls can sound like squeaks, grunts, groans, chirps, whistles, brays and growls. Add a squeaker to this little duck to make him talk.

Materials

24 Peg Small Gauge Knitting Loom

Yarn 3 or 4

20 yards for body and wings. 2 yards each for facial features. Red Heart was used in sample.

Tools/Notions

Knitting Pick

Tapestry Needle

Stuffing

Knee Highs or Pantyhose to contain stuffing – choose complimentary color to body of animal

Optional: 30 mm Bell or 1.5" Rattle Noise Maker

Gauge

4.5 st x 5 rows = 1"

Finished Size

Approximately 8" in diameter

BODY • • • • • • • • • • • • • • • • • •

DSCO 24 pegs, knit 20 rows in the round, use gather bo. Secure one end of body then stuff stocking and knot closed. Insert stocking into body. Gather the end of the body closed and secure yarn tail.

TOP BEAK

CO 6 pegs as flat panel

Row 1: slp k

Row 2: slp k

Row 3: slp k

Row 4: ssk, k2, k2tog

Row 5: k2tog, ssk

Row 6: ssk, pull through and snug

BOTTOM BEAK

CO 5 pegs as flat panel

Row 1: slp p

Row 2: slp p

Row 3: slp p

Row 4: p, p3tog, p

Row 5: p3tog, pull through and snug

WINGS: MAKE TWO

CO 7 pegs as flat panel

Row 1: slp k

Row 2: slp p

Row 3: slp k

Row 4: slp p

Row 5: slp k

Row 6: slp p

Row 7: slp, k, k2tog, k3 (6 pegs)

Row 8: slp, p, ssp, p2 (5 pegs)

Row 9: slp, k, k2tog, k3 (4 pegs)

Row 10: slp, p, ssp, p2 (3 pegs)

Bind off using basic BO, pull through and snug

ASSEMBLY ·

Using blue or black yarn, stitch the eyes in place using the method described in the notes section. Whip stitch the wings in place. Position the top beak in place and sew to body. Place the lower beak beneath the top beak so that they meet at the body, and sew in place. For the tuft, thread 10" piece of yarn through the top of head leaving a 1-2" end sticking out the top. Bring needle down through body and then back up to top – this will secure the middle part of the yarn. After yarn is back through the top again cut yarn the same length as the end sticking out. Using the needle, separate the ply of the yarn to fuzz it out some.

MOUSE

The word mouse means thief, and this little guy is sure to steal your heart away! He can be knit in many different colors for a whole "mischief" of mice.

Materials

24 Peg Small Gauge Knitting Loom

Yarn (3) or (4)

20 yards for body, ears and tail. 2 yards for facial features. Vanna's Choice was used in sample along with Peaches & Creme cotton.

Tools/Notions

Knitting Pick

Tapestry Needle

Stuffing

Knee Highs or Pantyhose to contain stuffing – choose complimentary color to body of animal

Optional: 30 mm Bell or 1.5" Rattle Noise Maker

Gauge

4.5 st x 5 rows = 1"

Finished Size

Approximately 8" in diameter

BODY •

DSCO 24 pegs, knit 20 rows in the round, use gather bo. Secure one end of body then stuff stocking as normal. Holding the stocking closed, insert stocking into body. Before knotting the stocking – roll some additional stuffing into a ball and put in the end of the stocking. This added stuffing and the stocking knot will form the nose of the mouse. Knot the end and push into the mouse body. Gather the end of the body closed and secure yarn tail.

EARS: MAKE 2

CO 5 pegs as flat panel

Row 1: k

Row 2: k, co 1

Row 3: k, co 1

Row 4: k, co 1

Row 5: k, co 1

Row 6: k3, k3tog, k3

Row 7: k2, k3tog, k2

Row 8: k, k3tog, k

Bind off using basic BO, pull through and snug

TAIL

Knit 4 peg i-cord until tail is 5-6" long.

ASSEMBLY

Take note of which end is more pointed at the gather closure and make sure to attach tail to the other end. Attach ears at top of head. Using pink yarn for nose and black yarn for the eyes, stitch in place using the method described in the notes section.

BEAR

Everyone loves a cute teddy bear. He would be nice knit up in a homespun yarn or a nice brown tweed. You have lots of color choices with this one.

Materials

24 Peg Small Gauge Knitting Loom

Yarn (3) or (4)

20 yards for body, muzzle and ears. 2 yards for facial features. Red Heart was used in sample.

Tools/Notions

Knitting Pick

Tapestry Needle

Stuffing

Knee Highs or Pantyhose to contain stuffing – choose complimentary color to body of animal

Optional: 30 mm Bell or 1.5" Rattle Noise Maker

Gauge

4.5 st x 5 rows = 1"

Finished Size

Approximately 8" in diameter

BODY

DSCO 24 pegs, knit 20 rows in the round, use gather bo. Secure one end of body then stuff stocking and knot closed. Insert stocking into body. Gather the end of the body closed and secure yarn tail.

EARS: MAKE 2

CO 5 pegs as flat panel

Row 1: k

Row 2: k, co 1

Row 3: k, co 1

Row 4: k, co 1

Row 5: k, co 1

Row 6: k2, k, k3tog, k, k2

Row 7: k1, k3tog, k1

Bind off using basic BO, pull through and snug

MUZZLE

Set up loom for 12 pegs in the round with sliders towards the center of loom (see photo.) DSCO 12 pegs in the round

Row 1-3: k

Row 4: move slider out, co new peg 1, knit 11 then co new peg, k1 (14 total pegs)

Row 5: k

Bind off using super stretchy bind off.

ASSEMBLY

Attach ears at top of head as shown in photo. Stitch muzzle in place using whip stitch. Using black yarn for eyes, nose and mouth, stitch in place using the method described in the notes section.

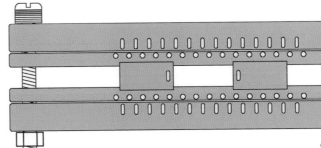

BUNNY

I used cotton yarn for this little cottontail to make him nice and soft. His fluffy pom pom tail makes him lots of fun.

Materials

24 Peg Small Gauge Knitting Loom

Yarn (3) or (4)

20 yards for body, ears and tail. 2 yards each for facial features. Peaches & Creme was used in sample.

Tools/Notions

Knitting Pick

Tapestry Needle

Stuffing

Knee Highs or Pantyhose to contain stuffing – choose complimentary color to body of animal

Optional: 30 mm Bell or 1.5" Rattle Noise Maker

Gauge

4.5 st x 5 rows = 1"

Finished Size

Approximately 8" in diameter

BODY

DSCO 24 pegs, knit 20 rows in the round, use gather bo. Secure one end of body then stuff stocking and knot closed. Insert stocking into body. Gather the end of the body closed and secure yarn tail.

TAIL

Make a pom-pom using two fingers on one hand and wrapping 12-20 times. Tie in the middle and cut outside edges. Using a needle, un-ply the yarn so that it has the ultimate fluffiness. A 4-ply cotton was used in the sample.

EARS: MAKE 2

CO 3 pegs as flat panel

Row 1: slp, k2, co 1

Row 2: slp, k3, co 1

Row 3: slp, k4, co 1

Row 4: slp, k5, co 1

Row 5: slp, k

Row 6: slp, k

Row 7: slp, k, k3tog, k2

Row 8: slp, k3tog, k

Bind off using basic BO, pull through and snug

ASSEMBLY

Attach ears at top of head and tail on back. Using blue yarn for eyes and pink yarn for nose and mouth stitch in place using the method described in the notes section.

PENGUIN

My son absolutely loves penguins, maybe even more than I do. No collection is complete without a "ping-ping" in it's midst.

BODY • • • • • • • • • • • • • • • •

DSCO 24 pegs, knit 20 rows in the round, use gather bo. Secure one end of body then stuff stocking and knot closed. Insert stocking into body. Gather the end of the body closed and secure yarn tail.

BEAK • • • • • • • • • • • • • • • •

CO 4 pegs as flat panel

Knit 4 rows. Bind off using basic BO, pull through and snug. Fold in half, knit side out and seam up the sides.

Materials

24 Peg Small Gauge Knitting Loom

Yarn (3) or (4)

20 yards for body and wings. 2 yards each for body features. Red Heart was used in sample.

Tools/Notions

Knitting Pick

Tapestry Needle

Stuffing

Knee Highs or Pantyhose to contain stuffing – choose complimentary color to body of animal

Optional: 30 mm Bell or 1.5" Rattle Noise Maker

Gauge

4.5 st x 5 rows = 1"

Finished Size

Approximately 8" in diameter

BELLY

CO 3 pegs as flat panel

Row 1: k, co 1

Row 2: k, co 1

Row 3: k, co 1

Row 4: k, co 1

Row 5: k

Row 6: k1, ssk, k1

Row 7: k1, k2tog, k1

Row 8: k1, k3tog, k1

Bind off using basic BO, pull through and snug.

WINGS: MAKE TWO

CO 5 pegs as flat panel

Row 1: p

Row 2: k

Row 3: p

Row 4: k

Row 5: p, co 1

Row 6: k

Row 7: p2tog, p

Row 8: k2, k2tog, k1

Row 9: p2tog, ssp

Row 10: ssk, pull through and snug

ASSEMBLY

Attach wings, belly, and beak using whip stitch as shown in photo. Using white or blue yarn for eyes stitch in place using the method described in the notes section.

ELEPHANT

This elephant pattern shows the versatility of the Kiss Looms by using just the peg board for the trunk. You can get a whole new gauge on the looms this way. Add a tuft of hair at the top if you like - see instructions for the duck.

Materials

24 Peg Small Gauge Knitting Loom

Yarn (3) or (4)

20 yards for body, ears and trunk. 2 yards for facial features. Red Heart was used in sample.

Tools/Notions

Knitting Pick

Tapestry Needle

Stuffing

Knee Highs or Pantyhose to contain stuffing – choose complimentary color to body of animal

Optional: 30 mm Bell or 1.5" Rattle Noise Maker

Gauge

4.5 st x 5 rows = 1"

Finished Size

Approximately 8" in diameter

BODY

DSCO 24 pegs, knit 20 rows in the round, use gather bo. Secure one end of body then stuff stocking and knot closed. Insert stocking into body. Gather the end of the body closed and secure yarn tail.

TRUNK

Remove pin board from loom and using only peg board CO 5 pegs and knit as a flat panel i-cord. See instructions in the notes section. Keep your stitches loose or they will get tight.

Row 1-10: k

Row 11: k, co 1

Row 12: k, co 1

Row 13-20: k

Bind off using gather BO, pull snug. Pull on both ends and twist until slack is removed and you achieve a smooth knit on all sides.

EARS: MAKE 2 ••

CO 4 pegs as flat panel

Row 1: p, co1

Row 2: k

Row 3: p, co1

Row 4: k

Row 5: p, co1

Row 6: k

Row 7: p, co1

Row 8: k, co1

Row 9: p

Row 10: k

Row 11: p6, ssp, p1

Row 12: k

Row 13: p5, ssp, p1

Row 14: k4, k2tog, k1

Row 15: p1, p2tog, ssp, p1

Bind off using basic BO, pull through and snug

ASSEMBLY · · · · · · · · ·

Attach ears at side of head and wider end of nose in the middle of the front. Using black yarn for eyes stitch in place using the method described in the notes section.

LADYBUG

I just love this ladybug; I can picture her peeking out of a basket on Easter morning. She's got a lot of personality. You can add as many dots on the wings as you like. Ladybugs are actually born without spots and can develop up to 20.

Materials

24 Peg Small Gauge Knitting Loom

Yarn (3) or (4)

20 yards each for body and wings. 2 yards each for facial and wing features. Red Heart was used in sample.

Tools/Notions

Knitting Pick

Tapestry Needle

Stuffing

Knee Highs or Pantyhose to contain stuffing – choose complimentary color to body of animal

Optional: 30 mm Bell or 1.5" Rattle Noise Maker

Gauge

4.5 st x 5 rows = 1"

Finished Size

Approximately 8" in diameter

BODY • • • • • • • • • • • • • • • • • •

DSCO 24 pegs, knit 20 rows in the round, use gather bo. Secure one end of body then stuff stocking lightly and knot closed. Insert stocking into body. Gather the end of the body closed and secure yarn tail.

WINGS: MAKE 2

CO 9 pegs as flat panel

Row 1: slp k

Row 2: slp p

Row 3: slp k

Row 4: slp p

Row 5: slp k

Row 6: slp p

Row 7: slp k

Row 8: slp p

Row 9: slp, k, k2tog, k5 (8 pegs)

Row 10: slp, p, ssp, p4 (7 pegs)

Repeat rows 9 and 10 until three stitches remain and row is ko

Bind off using basic BO, pull through and snug.

SPOTS

Stitch 3 spots on each wing. Then holding the two wings together, stitch one larger spot across both wings at the top as shown in the picture.

ANTENNA: MAKE TWO

Do a crochet chain stitch about 1.5" long. Tie a knot in one end for the top of the antenna. See notes for chain stitch instructions.

ASSEMBLY

Flatten body out to a disc shape. Attach approximately 1" of the wings to the back of the body along head edge. Using white or light grey yarn for eyes and head spots stitch in place using the method described in the notes section. Attach antenna to the top of head.

RACCOON

This cute little rascal was suggested by Cliff, inventor of Kiss Looms. He is a great addtion to the dot collection and turned out even better than I imagined.

Materials

24 Peg Small Gauge Knitting Loom

Yarn (3) or (4)

20 yards for body, ears and tail. 2 yards each for facial features. Red Heart was used in sample.

Tools/Notions

Knitting Pick

Tapestry Needle

Stuffing

Knee Highs or Pantyhose to contain stuffing – choose complimentary color to body of animal

Optional: 30 mm Bell or 1.5" Rattle Noise Maker

Gauge

4.5 st x 5 rows = 1"

Finished Size

Approximately 8" in diameter

BODY • • • • • • • • • • • • • • • • •

DSCO 24 pegs, knit 20 rows in the round, use gather bo. Secure one end of body then stuff stocking lightly and knot closed. Insert stocking into body. Gather the end of the body closed and secure yarn tail.

Cliff Roush
Inventor of Kiss Looms

Cliff was an amazing man and one of my best friends. He and I met in 2009 and instantly knew that we were two peas in a pod. We often finished each others sentences and spoke nearly every day. He has changed so many lives with his looms and brought so many people together that would have never met otherwise. He loved being involved with Kiss Looms and all the wonderful knitters across the country and world. I hope to do my very best to keep his legacy alive.

WHITE EYE PATCH: MAKE TWO

CO 7 pegs as flat panel

Row 1: slp k

Row 2: slp p

Row 3: slp k

Row 4: slp p

Row 5: slp k

Row 6: slp p

Row 7: k2tog, k2tog k3 (5 pegs)

Row 8: slp, p, p2tog, p (4 pegs)

Row 9: slp, k, ssk (3 pegs)

Bind off using basic purl BO, pull through and snug.

GREY EYE PATCH

Stitch in place on white eye patch with photo as a guide. Use method described in the notes section. Stitch black eye in place using photo for reference on placement.

EARS: MAKE TWO

CO 6 pegs as flat panel

Row 1: slp, k

Row 2: slp, k

Row 3: k2tog, k2, ssk

Row 4: ssk, k2tog

Row 5: k2tog, pull through and snug

TAIL

DSCO 14 pegs in the round

Row 1-4: knit in black

Row 5-9: knit in gray

Repeat till you have three sections of each color and finish with a gray stripe.

Bind off using super stretchy bind off.

ASSEMBLY

Flatten body out to a disc shape. Attach white eye patch with gray patch and eye already sewn, to body. Stitch nose in place between the two white eye patches. Sew ears in place on top of body. Hold tail bind off edges to body making sure to form it around the body slightly - stitch the tail in place. Tail should not be sewn closed against the body – it should be rounded slightly to meet the shape of the body.

FROG

This little dot was my third creation in this series and probably one of the simplist of the bunch. I hope you enjoy his cute froggy smile as much as I do.

Materials

24 Peg Small Gauge Knitting Loom

Yarn (3) or (4)

20 yards for body. 2 yards each for facial features. I Love This Yarn was used in sample.

Tools/Notions

Knitting Pick

Tapestry Needle

Stuffing

Knee Highs or Pantyhose to contain stuffing – choose complimentary color to body of animal

Optional: 30 mm Bell or 1.5" Rattle Noise Maker

Gauge

4.5 st x 5 rows = 1"

Finished Size

Approximately 8" in diameter

BODY •

DSCO 24 pegs, knit 20 rows in the round, gather bo. Secure one end of body then stuff stocking and knot closed. Insert stocking into body. Gather the end of the body closed and secure yarn tail.

EYES: MAKE TWO • • • • • • • • • • •

CO 8 pegs in the round, knit 6 rows, gather bo.

ASSEMBLY

Using black yarn stitch the eyeballs in place on the white eyes, and the nostrils and mouth in place using the method described in the notes section. Lightly stuff the eyes and sew in place on top of the head - they should be rounded slightly at the bottom to meet the shape of the body.

TIGER/CAT

This tiger was one of my first dot projects. I think in a lot of ways he looks like a cat so feel free to leave off the stripes or knit him in any variety of colors.

Materials

24 Peg Small Gauge Knitting Loom

Yarn (3) or (4)

20 yards each for body, ears and tail. 2 yards for facial features. Red Heart was used in sample.

Tools/Notions

Knitting Pick

Tapestry Needle

Stuffing

Knee Highs or Pantyhose to contain stuffing – choose complimentary color to body of animal

Optional: 30 mm Bell or 1.5" Rattle Noise Maker

Gauge

4.5 st x 5 rows = 1"

Finished Size

Approximately 8" in diameter

BODY • • • • • • • • • • • • • • • • • •

CO 24 pegs using DSCO for flat panel (see notes section), knit 20 rows as a flat panel using the following pattern - knit 8 pegs in orange at the beginning of each row then knit the remaining pegs in the following pattern (see pic): 2 rows orange, 2 rows black, repeat until you have 20 rows. Do not cut yarn between color changes – bring it up the side. See note about how to change colors mid row. Use flat panel gather bo, seam sides. Stuff stocking and knot closed. Insert stocking into body. Gather the end of the body closed and secure yarn tail.

TAIL

Knit 4 peg i-cord with 4 rows in orange, *2 rows black, 2 rows orange, repeat from * until tail is 5" long. Do not cut yarn between color changes - carry it to the middle of the i-cord.

EARS: MAKE TWO

CO 5 pegs as flat panel

Row 1: slp, k

Row 2: slp, k

Row 3: slp, k, p, k, k

Row 4: slp, k, p, k, k

Row 5: k2tog, p, ssk

Row 6: slp, k, k

Row 7: k3tog, pull loop through and snug

Stretch ears side to side a little to round them out and tuck in tail to round out top.

ASSEMBLY

Using pink yarn for nose and black yarn for the eyes and mouth stitch in place using the method described in the notes section. Attach ears at top of head along the stripe line and attach tail to back near the bottom – make sure it won't hinder it sitting up.

BEE

Another one of my favorites. He just came out with such personality. Don't upset him though - that stinger packs quite a wallop!

Materials

24 Peg Small Gauge Knitting Loom

Yarn (3) or (4)

20 yards each for body and facial features. Red Heart was used in sample.

Tools/Notions

Knitting Pick

Tapestry Needle

Stuffing

Knee Highs or Pantyhose to contain stuffing – choose complimentary color to body of animal

Optional: 30 mm Bell or 1.5" Rattle Noise Maker

Gauge

4.5 st x 5 rows = 1"

Finished Size

Approximately 8" in diameter

BODY • • • • • • • • • • • • • • • • • •

CO 24 pegs using DSCO for flat panel (see notes section), knit 20 rows as a flat panel, using the following pattern - 4 rows yellow, 2 rows black, 3 rows yellow, 2 rows black, 3 rows yellow, 2 rows black, 2 rows yellow, 2 rows black. Do not cut yarn between color changes – bring it up the side. Use a flat panel gather bo, seam sides. Stuff stocking and knot closed. Insert stocking into body. Gather the end of the body closed and secure yarn tail.

ANTENNA: MAKE TWO

CO 3 pegs right to left, work 3 peg flat stitch i-cord for 4 rows in yellow, place black yarn slip knot on peg 3, then co peg 4 in black and work 4 peg ew i-cord in black for 3 rows.

STINGER

CO 3 pegs and work 3 peg flat stitch i-cord for 7 rows in black, then k3tog, pull through and snug.

ASSEMBLY

Attach stinger to the black end of the bee and antenna to yellow end. Using black yarn stitch the eyes and mouth in place using the method described in the notes section.

LION

This lion is what started it all! A friend asked if I could make a knitted animal for a baby shower with a jungle theme, and away I went! This one is especially easy for little hands to grab the mane and tail.

Materials

24 Peg Small Gauge Knitting Loom

Yarn (3) or (4)

25 yards for body, muzzle, tail and mane. 2 yards each for facial features. Vanna's Choice was used in sample.

Tools/Notions

Knitting Pick

Tapestry Needle

Stuffing

Knee Highs or Pantyhose to contain stuffing – choose complimentary color to body of animal

Optional: 30 mm Bell or 1.5" Rattle Noise Maker

Gauge

4.5 st x 5 rows = 1"

Finished Size

Approximately 8" in diameter

BODY •

DSCO 24 pegs, knit 20 rows in the round, use gather bo. Secure one end of body then stuff stocking and knot closed. Insert stocking into body. Gather the end of the body closed and secure yarn tail.

MANE

Knit 3 peg flat stitch i-cord approximately 36" to fit around 8.5" diameter ball. You can knit extra length and pull it from the loom without doing a bind off to make sure you have enough. After sewing it on you can pull out any extra rows and use the tail to thread through each loop sticking up to gather that end closed.

MUZZLE

Set up the loom for 12 pegs in the round with sliders towards the center of loom (see photo on bear pattern.) DSCO 12 pegs in the round

Row 1-3: k

Row 4: move slider out, co new peg 1, knit 11 then co new peg, k1 (14 total pegs)

Row 5: k

BO with super stretchy bind off

TAIL

Knit 4 peg flat stitch i-cord until tail is 5-6" long.

ASSEMBLY

Loop i-cord and stitch in place a little at a time – make sure you have enough to go around the entire ball. I-cord should be stitched slightly to the front edge of the ball instead of centered around ball. Lightly stuff muzzle and stitch in place. Using black (or other) and pink yarn stitch the eyes, mouth and nose in place using the method described in the notes section. Stitch tail in place and tie knot in end if desired.

BIRD

This little bird was featured in the Loom Knitters Circle E-Magazine in the fall 2012 issue. He was knit in a soft durable cotton and can be made in so many different colors.

BODY · · · · · · · · · · · · · · · · · · ·

DSCO 24 pegs, knit 20 rows in the round, use gather bo. Secure one end of body then stuff stocking and knot closed. Insert stocking into body. Gather the end of the body closed and secure yarn tail.

Materials

24 Peg Small Gauge Knitting Loom

Yarn (3) or (4)

20 yards for body and wings. 2 yards each for facial features. Peaches & Creme was used in sample.

Tools/Notions

Knitting Pick

Tapestry Needle

Stuffing

Knee Highs or Pantyhose to contain stuffing – choose complimentary color to body of animal

Optional: 30 mm Bell or 1.5" Rattle Noise Maker

Gauge

4.5 st x 5 rows = 1"

Finished Size

Approximately 8" in diameter

BEAK

CO 3 pegs as flat panel, left to right

Row 1: knit right to left

Row 2: take yarn around back to peg 1 - knit right to left

move peg 1 to 2 and 3 to 2 - wrap and knit off - pull yarn through and snug

pull on beginning tail to close i-cord

WINGS: MAKE TWO

CO 7 pegs as flat panel

Row 1: slp knit

Row 2: slp purl

Row 3: slp knit

Row 4: slp purl

Row 5: slp knit

Row 6: slp purl

Row 7: slp, k, k2tog, k3 (6 pegs)

Row 8: slp, p, ssp, p2 (5 pegs)

Repeat rows 7 and 8 till three stitches remain

BO by wrapping peg two, knit off - move loop to 1st peg knit off, move 1st peg over, wrap peg 3 knit off, move to 2nd peg knit off, wrap once more than knit off, pull through and snug

ASSEMBLY

Using black (or other) yarn stitch the eyes in place using method described in the notes section. Attach the beak and wings as shown in photo.

PIG

Materials

24 Peg Small Gauge Knitting Loom

Yarn (3) or (4)

20 yards for body, ears, muzzle and tail. 2 yards for facial features. Red Heart was used in sample.

Tools/Notions

Knitting Pick

Tapestry Needle

Stuffing

Knee Highs or Pantyhose to contain stuffing – choose complimentary color to body of animal

Optional: 30 mm Bell or 1.5" Rattle Noise Maker

Gauge

4.5 st x 5 rows = 1"

Finished Size

Approximately 8" in diameter

Pigs can have straight and curly tails. Some say they are happy when their tail is curly. Give this little guy a curly tail and you'll both be happy!

BODY • • • • • • • • • • • • • • • • • •

DSCO 24 pegs, knit 20 rows in the round, use gather bo. Secure one end of body then stuff stocking and knot closed. Insert stocking into body. Gather the end of the body closed and secure yarn tail.

TAIL • • • • • • • • • • • • • • • • • •

Knit a 3 peg flat stitch i-cord 3.5" long

EARS: MAKE TWO

CO 5 pegs as flat panel

Row 1: p

Row 2: k

Row 3: p, co 1

Row 4: k

Row 5: p2tog, p

Row 6: k2, ssk, k1

Row 7: p2tog, ssp

Row 8: ssk, pull through and snug

NOSE

CO 10 pegs in the round left to right

Row 1-2: k

Row 3: ssk, ssk, k2, ssk, ssk (6 pegs) – move loops first – peg 1 to 2, peg 3 to 4 then move these loops back to peg 3, don't move pegs 5 and 6, move 7 to 8 and 9 to 10. Move loop 6 to 7 then push sliders in and knit the round

Row 4: ssk (3x) (3 pegs.) For this one it is easiest to move the loop then knit, move the next loop then knit. Loops will be in a triangle from each other – don't worry about the gap

Row 5: move loop furthest from working yarn to center peg then the loop with working yarn – k3tog, pull through and snug

ASSEMBLY

Stuff nose a little and sew onto one of the drawstring ends of the ball. It should be rounded slightly to meet the shape of the body. Using black yarn stitch the eyes, nostrils and mouth in place using the method described in the notes section. Attach ears to top of head area. Curl tail into a curly-q and using one of the tails, stitch back and forth through the cord until it's shaped. Attach tail to back of pig.

DRAGON

This dragon pattern was orginally a pair of slippers I designed a few years ago and as I was looking for the final pattern in the book they kept coming to mind and I just had to do a "dot" dragon pattern too. Hope you like him.

BODY ••••••••••••••••••••••••••••

DSCO 24 pegs, knit 20 rows in the round, use gather bo. Secure one end of body then stuff stocking lightly and knot closed. Insert stocking into body. Gather the end of the body closed and secure yarn tail.

Materials
24 Peg Small Gauge Knitting Loom

Yarn (3) or (4)
20 yards for body and tail. 15 yards for wings and facial features. Red Heart was used in sample.

Tools/Notions
Knitting Pick

Tapestry Needle

Stuffing

Knee Highs or Pantyhose to contain stuffing – choose complimentary color to body of animal

Optional: 30 mm Bell or 1.5" Rattle Noise Maker

Gauge
4.5 st x 5 rows = 1"

Finished Size
Approximately 8" in diameter

WINGS: MAKE TWO •

CO 10 pegs as flat panel

Row 1: slp, p

Row 2: slp, k

Row 3: p2tog, p (9 pegs)

Row 4: slp, k6, k2tog (8 pegs)

Row 5: slp, p

Row 6: slp, k7, co1 (9 pegs)

Row 7: p

Row 8: slp, k6, k2tog (8 pegs)

Row 9: p2tog, p6, co1 (8 pegs)

Row 10: slp, k

Row 11: p2tog, p (7 pegs)

Row 12: slp, k4, k2tog, co2 (8 pegs)

Row 13: p8, co1 (9 pegs)

Row 14: slp, k

Row 15: p2tog, p2, p2tog, p3 (7 pegs)

Row 16: ssk, k2, ssk, k (5 pegs)

Row 17: p2tog, p, p2tog (3 pegs)

Row 18: ssk, k (2 pegs)

Row 19: p2tog (1 peg)

Row 20: k pull through and snug

TAIL

CO 4 pegs left to right as flat panel, work a flat panel i-cord for 7 rows

You will be breaking the i-cord starting on row 8 - do not bring the yarn around the back! Knit back and forth as normal.

Row 8: knit left to right co 1

Row 9: knit right to left co1

Row 10: knit left to right co1

Row 11: knit right to left co1

Row 12: k3, ssk, k3

Row 13: k2, k3tog, k2

Row 14: k1, k3tog, k1

Row 15: k3tog

Row 16: k1 pull through and snug

ASSEMBLY

Flatten body out to a disc shape. Attach wings and tail to body. Using same color as the wings, stitch eyes and mouth in place using the method described in the notes section.

Acknowledgments

There are so many people I want to thank for helping me to get through this project. I have had so much encouragement from the loom knitting community that it overwhelms me. Special thanks go out to my helpers for this project – Graciela Worth and Kathy Bouras who pushed me daily to work on it when I really needed the motivation to keep plugging along. Linda and Carol who were my new loomer sounding boards for the patterns and instructions.

To Bethany Daily and Brenda Myers for your great support and help with my questions as I figured out how to make this book happen. My amazing neighbor Laura who helped proof the book and was always nice enough to look at my newest creation the minute I got it done. My mom and dad who were a big encouragement to me and always wanted to see my new creations and dad who was able to take my rambling illustration ideas and turn them into something nice.

To my husband and wonderful kids, I could not have done this without you. You guys are my inspiration in everything! Thanks for being patient with me while I got this done. Darryl, you are the best husband and personal graphic designer a woman could ask for! You took my idea and really pushed me to make it the best it could be. With you behind me, how could I fail. Thank you for all your hard work on this, it turned out so beautiful! Isaiah thank you for your great ideas for some of the "dots" and "oohs and ahhs" when I got one done. Ruth I love how you've snuggled and played with them, sometimes before I could even get pictures taken!

Finally to Cliff and Sherrie, you guys are also the authors of my inspiration with your wonderful looms and love and support. Cliff I wish you could have been here to see me finish. Thank you Sherrie for your continued friendship. You will always be a part of my family.

Links

http://kisslooms.com

http://groups.yahoo.com/group/Kiss-looms/

http://kellyknits.com

http://gracielandcrafts.typepad.com/

http://loomknittingmeme.blogspot.com/

http://gettinitpegged.com/

http://loomlady.blogspot.com/

29330726R00046

Made in the USA
Lexington, KY
23 January 2014